An account of

trade on the coast of Africa

Alexander Falconbridge

Alpha Editions

This edition published in 2024

ISBN : 9789362990532

Design and Setting By
Alpha Editions
www.alphaedis.com
Email - info@alphaedis.com

Contents

PREFACE.

The following sheets are intended to lay before the public the present state of a branch of the British commerce, which, ever since its existence, has been held in detestation by all good men, but at this time more particularly engages the attention of the nation, and is become the object of general reprobation.

Leaving to abler pens to expatiate more at large on the injustice and inhumanity of the *Slave Trade*, I shall content myself with giving some account of the hardships which the unhappy objects of it undergo, and the cruelties they suffer, from the period of their being reduced to a state of slavery, to their being disposed of in the West India islands; where, I fear, their grievances find little alleviation. At the same time, I shall treat of a subject, which appears not to have been attended to in the manner its importance requires; that is, the sufferings and loss of the seamen employed in this trade; which, from the intemperature of the climate, the inconveniencies they labour under during the voyage, and the severity of most of the commanders, occasion the destruction of great numbers annually.

And this I shall endeavour to do by the recital of a number of facts which have fallen under my own immediate observation, or the knowledge of which I have obtained from persons on whose veracity I can depend.

And happy shall I esteem myself, if an experience obtained by a series of inquiries and observations, made during several voyages to the coast of Africa, shall enable me to render any service to a cause, which is become the cause of every person of humanity.

Before I proceed to the methods of obtaining the slaves, and their subsequent treatment, the treatment of the sailors, and a concise account of the places on the coast of Africa where slaves are obtained, (which I purpose to annex,) it may not be unnecessary to give a short sketch of the usual proceedings of the ships employed in the slave trade.

AN
ACCOUNT
OF THE
SLAVE TRADE, &c.

Proceedings during the Voyage.

On the arrival of the ships at Bonny, and New Calabar, it is customary for them to unbend the sails, strike the yards and topmasts, and begin to build what they denominate *a house*. This is effected in the following manner. The sailors first lash the booms and yards from mast to mast, in order to form a *ridge-pole*. About ten feet above the deck, several spars, equal in length to the ridge pole, are next lashed to the standing rigging, and form a wall-plate. Across the ridge-pole and wall-plate, several other spars or rafters are afterwards laid and lashed, at the distance of about six inches from each other. On these, other rafters or spars are laid length-wise, equal in extent to the ridge-pole, so as to form a kind of lattice or net-work, with interfaces of six inches square. The roof is then covered with mats, made of rushes of very loose texture, fastened together with rope-yarn, and so placed, as to lap over each other like tiles. The space between the deck and the wall-plate, is likewise enclosed with a kind of lattice, or net-work, formed of sticks, lashed across each other, and leaving vacancies of about four inches square. Near the main-mast, a partition is constructed of inch deal boards, which reaches athwart the ship. This division is called a *barricado*. It is about eight feet in height, and is made to project near two feet over the sides of the ship. In this barricado there is a door, at which a centinel is placed during the time the negroes are permitted to come upon deck. It serves to keep the different sexes apart; and as there are small holes in it, wherein blunderbusses are fixed, and sometimes a cannon, it is found very convenient for quelling the insurrections that now and then happen. Another door is made in the lattice or net-work at the ladder, by which you enter the ship. This door is guarded by a centinel during the day, and is locked at night. At the head of the ship there is a third door, for the use of the sailors, which is secured in the same manner as that at the gangway. There is also in the roof a large trap-door, through which the goods intended for barter, the water casks, &c. are hoisted out or in.

The design of this house is to secure those on board from the heat of the sun, which in this latitude is intense, and from the wind and rain, which at particular seasons, are likewise extremely violent. It answers these purposes however but very ineffectually. The slight texture of the mats admits both the wind and the rain, whenever it happens to be violent, though at the same time, it increases the heat of the ship to a very pernicious degree, especially between decks. The increased warmth occasioned by this means, together with the smoke produced from the green mangrove, (the usual firewood) which, for want of a current of air to carry it off, collects itself in large quantities, and infests every part of the ship, render a vessel during its stay here very unhealthy. The smoke also, by its acrimonious quality, often produces inflammations in the eyes, which terminates sometimes in the loss of sight.

Another purpose for which these temporary houses are erected, is, in order to prevent the purchased negroes from leaping overboard. This, the horrors of their situation frequently impel them to attempt; and they now and then effect it, notwithstanding all the precautions that are taken, by forcing their way through the lattice work.

The slave ships generally lie near a mile below the town, in Bonny River, in seven or eight fathom water. Sometimes fifteen sail, English and French, but chiefly the former, meet here together. Soon after they cast anchor, the captains go on shore, to make known their arrival, and to inquire into the state of the trade. They likewise invite the kings of Bonny to come on board, to whom, previous to breaking bulk, they usually make presents (in that country termed *dashes*) which generally consist of pieces of cloth, cotton, chintz, silk handkerchiefs, and other India goods, and sometimes of brandy, wine, or beer.

When I was at Bonny a few years ago, it was the residence of two kings, whose names were *Norfolk* and *Peppel*. The houses of these princes were not distinguished from the cottages or huts of which the town consists, in any other manner, than by being of somewhat larger dimensions, and surrounded with warehouses containing European goods, designed for the purchase of slaves. These slaves, which the kings procure in the same manner as the black traders do theirs, are sold by them to the ships. And for every negroe sold there by the traders, the kings receive a duty, which amounts to a considerable sum in the course of a year. This duty is collected by officers, stationed on board the ships, who are termed *officer boys*; a denomination which it is thought they received from the English.

The kings of Bonny are absolute, though elective. They are assisted in the government by a small number of persons of a certain rank, who stile themselves *parliament gentlemen*; an office which they generally hold for life. Every ship, on its arrival, is expected to send a present to these gentlemen, of a small quantity of bread and beef, and likewise to treat them as often as they come on board. When they do this, their approach to the ship is announced by blowing through a hollow elephant's tooth, which produces a sound resembling that of a post-horn.

After the kings have been on board, and have received the usual presents, permission is granted by them, for trafficking with any of the black traders. When the royal guests return from the ships, they are saluted by the guns.

From the time of the arrival of the ships to their departure, which is usually near three months, scarce a day passes without some negroes being purchased, and carried on board; sometimes in small, and sometimes in larger numbers. The whole number taken on board, depends, in a great measure, on circumstances. In a voyage I once made, our stock of merchandize was exhausted in the purchase of about 380 negroes, which was expected to have procured 500. The number of English and French ships then at Bonny, had so far raised the price of negroes, as to occasion this difference.

The reverse (and a *happy* reverse I think I may call it) was known during the late war. When I was last at Bonny, I frequently made inquiries on this head, of one of the black traders, whose intelligence I believe I can depend upon. He informed me that only one ship had been there for three years during that period; and that was the *Moseley-Hill*, Captain Ewing, from Liverpool, who made an extraordinary purchase, as he found negroes remarkably cheap from the dulness of trade. Upon further inquiring of my black acquaintance, what was the consequence of this decay of their trade, he shrugged up his shoulders, and answered, *only making us traders poorer, and obliging us to work for our maintenance.* One of these black merchants being informed, that a particular set of people, called Quakers, were for abolishing the trade, he said, *it was a very bad thing, as they should then be reduced to the same state they were in during the war, when, through poverty, they were obliged to dig the ground and plant yams.*

I was once upon the coast of Angola also, when there had not been a slave ship at the river Ambris for five years previous to our arrival, although a place to which many usually resort every year; and the failure of the trade for that period, as far as we could learn, had not any other effect, than to restore peace and confidence among the natives; which, upon the arrival of any ships, is immediately destroyed, by the inducement then held forth in the purchase of slaves. And during the suspension of trade at Bonny, as above-mentioned, none of the dreadful proceedings, which are so confidently asserted to be the natural consequence of it, were known. The reduction of the price of negroes, and the poverty of the black traders, appear to have been the only *bad* effects of the discontinuance of trade; the *good* ones were, *most probably,* the restoration of peace and confidence among the natives, and a suspension of kidnapping.

When the ships have disposed of all their merchandize in the purchase of negroes, and have laid in their stock of wood, water, and yams, they prepare for sailing, by getting up the yards and topmasts, reeving the running rigging, bending the sails, and by taking down the temporary house. They then drop down the river, to wait for a favourable opportunity to pass over the bar, which is formed by a number of sand-banks lying across the mouth of the river, with navigable channels between them. It is not uncommon for ships to get upon the bar, and sometimes they are lost.

The first place the slave ships touch at in their passage to the West-Indies, is either the Island of St. Thomas, or Princes Island, where they usually carry their sick on shore, for the benefit of the air, and likewise replenish their stock of water. The former of these islands is nearly circular, being one hundred and twenty miles round, and lies exactly under the equator, about forty-five leagues from the African continent. It abounds with wood and water, and produces Indian corn, rice, fruits, sugar, and some cinnamon. The air is rather prejudicial to an European constitution, nevertheless it is well peopled by the Portuguese. Princes Island, which is much smaller, lies in 1 deg. 30 min. north latitude, and likewise produces Indian corn, and a variety of fruits and roots, besides sugar canes. Black cattle, hogs, and goats are numerous there; but it is infested with a mischievous and dangerous species of monkeys.

During one of the voyages I made, I was landed upon the Island of St. Thomas, with near one hundred sick negroes, who were placed in an old house, taken on purpose for their reception. Little benefit however accrued from their going on shore, as several of them died there, and the remainder continued nearly in the same situation as when they were landed, though our continuance was prolonged for about twelve days, and the island is deemed upon the whole healthy.

Upon the arrival of the slave ships in the West-Indies, a day is soon fixed for the sale of their cargoes. And this is done by different modes, and often by one they term a *scramble*, of which some account will be given, when the sale of the negroes is treated of.

The whole of their cargoes being disposed of, the ships are immediately made ready to proceed to sea. It is very seldom, however, that they are not detained, for want of a sufficient number of sailors to navigate the ship, as this trade may justly be denominated the grave of seamen. Though the crews of the ships upon their leaving England, generally amount to between forty and fifty men, scarcely three-fourths, and sometimes not one-third of the complement, ever return to the port from whence they sailed, through mortality and desertion; the causes of which I shall speak of under another head.

The time during which the slave ships are absent from England, varies according to the destination of the voyage, and the number of ships they happen to meet on the coast. To Bonny, or Old and New Calabar, a voyage is usually performed in about ten months. Those to the Windward and Gold Coasts, are rather more uncertain, but in general from fifteen to eighteen months.

The Manner in which the Slaves are procured.

After permission has been obtained for *breaking trade*, as it is termed, the captains go ashore, from time to time, to examine the negroes that are exposed to sale, and to make their purchases. The unhappy wretches thus disposed of, are bought by the black traders at fairs, which are held for that purpose, at the distance of upwards of two hundred miles from the sea coast; and these fairs are said to be supplied from an interior part of the country. Many negroes, upon being questioned relative to the places of their nativity have asserted, that they have travelled during the revolution of several moons, (their usual method of calculating time) before they have reached the places where they were purchased by the black traders. At these fairs, which are held at uncertain periods, but generally every six weeks, several thousands are frequently exposed to sale, who had been collected from all parts of the country for a very considerable distance round. While I was upon the coast, during one of the voyages I made, the black traders brought down, in different canoes, from twelve to fifteen hundred negroes, which had been purchased at one fair. They consisted chiefly of men and boys, the women seldom exceeding a third of the whole number. From forty to two hundred negroes are generally purchased at a time by the black traders, according to the opulence of the buyer; and consist of those of all ages, from a month, to sixty years and upwards. Scarce any age or situation is deemed an exception, the price being proportionable. Women sometimes form a part of them, who happen to be so far advanced in their pregnancy, as to be delivered during their journey from the fairs to the coast; and I have frequently seen instances of deliveries on board ship. The slaves purchased at these fairs are only for the supply of the markets at Bonny, and Old and New Calabar.

There is great reason to believe, that most of the negroes shipped off from the coast of Africa, are *kidnapped*. But the extreme care taken by the black traders to prevent the Europeans from gaining any intelligence of their modes of proceeding; the great distance inland from whence the negroes are brought; and our ignorance of their language, (with which, very frequently, the black traders themselves are equally unacquainted) prevent our obtaining such information on this head as we could wish. I have, however, by means of occasional inquiries, made through interpreters, procured some intelligence relative to the point, and such, as I think, puts the matter beyond a doubt.

From these I shall select the following striking instances:—While I was in employ on board one of the slave ships, a negroe informed me, that being one evening invited to drink with some of the black traders, upon his going away, they attempted to seize him. As he was very active, he evaded their design, and got out of their hands. He was however prevented from effecting his escape by a large dog, which laid hold of him, and compelled him to submit. These creatures are kept by many of the traders for that purpose; and being trained to the inhuman sport, they appear to be much pleased with it.

I was likewise told by a negroe woman, that as she was on her return home, one evening, from some neighbours, to whom she had been making a visit by invitation, she was kidnapped; and, notwithstanding she was big with child, sold for a slave. This transaction happened a considerable way up the country, and she had passed through the hands of several purchasers before she reached the ship. A man and his son, according to their own information, were seized by professed kidnappers, while they were planting yams, and sold for slaves. This likewise happened in the interior parts of the country, and after passing through several hands, they were purchased for the ship to which I belonged.

It frequently happens, that those who kidnap others, are themselves, in their turns, seized and sold. A negroe in the West-Indies informed me, that after having been employed in kidnapping others, he had experienced this reverse. And he assured me, that it was a common incident among his countrymen.

Continual enmity is thus fostered among the negroes of Africa, and all social intercourse between them destroyed; which most assuredly would not be the case, had they not these opportunities of finding a ready sale for each other.

During my stay on the coast of Africa, I was an eye-witness of the following transaction:——A black trader invited a negroe, who resided a little way up the country, to come and see him. After the entertainment was over, the trader proposed to his guest, to treat him with a sight of one of the ships lying in the river. The unsuspicious countryman readily consented, and accompanied the trader in a canoe to the side of the ship, which he viewed with pleasure and astonishment. While he was thus employed, some black traders on board, who appeared to be in the secret, leaped into the canoe, seized the unfortunate man, and dragging him into the ship, immediately sold him.

Previous to my being in this employ, I entertained a belief, as many others have done, that the kings and principal men *breed* negroes for sale, as we do cattle. During the different times I was in the country, I took no little pains to satisfy myself in this particular; but notwithstanding I made many inquiries, I was not able to obtain the least intelligence of this being the case, which it is more than probable I should have done, had such a practice prevailed. All the information I could procure, confirms me in the belief, that to *kidnapping*, and to crimes, (and many of these fabricated as a pretext) the slave trade owes its chief support.

The following instance tends to prove, that the last mentioned artifice is often made use of. Several black traders, one of whom was a person of consequence, and exercised an authority somewhat similar to that of our magistrates, being in want of some particular kind of merchandize, and not having a slave to barter for it, they accused a fisherman, at the river Ambris, with extortion in the sale of his fish; and as they were interested in the decision, they immediately adjudged the poor fellow guilty, and condemned him to be sold. He was accordingly purchased by the ship to which I belonged, and brought on board.

As an additional proof that kidnapping is not only the general, but almost the sole mode, by which slaves are procured, the black traders, in purchasing them, chuse those which are the roughest and most hardy; alleging, that the smooth negroes have been *gentlemen*. By this observation we may conclude they mean that nothing but fraud or force could have reduced these smooth-skinned gentlemen to a state of slavery.

It may not be here unworthy of remark, in order to prove that the wars among the Africans do not furnish the number of slaves they are supposed to do, that I never saw any negroes with recent wounds; which must have been the consequence, at least with some of them, had they been taken in battle. And it being the particular province of the surgeon to examine the slaves when they are purchased, such a circumstance could not have escaped my observation. As a farther corroboration, it might be remarked, that on the Gold and Windward Coasts, where fairs are not held, the number of slaves procured at a time are usually very small.

The preparations made at Bonny by the black traders, upon setting out for the fairs which are held up the country, are very considerable. From twenty to thirty canoes, capable of containing thirty or forty negroes each, are assembled for this purpose; and such goods put on board them as they expect will be wanted for the purchase of the number of slaves they intend to buy. When their loading is completed, they commence their voyage, with colours flying and musick playing; and in about ten or eleven days, they generally return to Bonny with full cargoes. As soon as the canoes arrive at the trader's landing-place, the purchased negroes are cleaned, and oiled with palm oil; and on the following day they are exposed for sale to the captains.

The black traders do not always purchase their slaves at the same rate. The speed with which the information of the arrival of ships upon the coast is conveyed to the fairs, considering it is the interest of the traders to keep them ignorant, is really surprising. In a very short time after any ships arrive upon the coast, especially if several make their appearance together, those who dispose of the negroes at the fairs are frequently known to increase the price of them.

These fairs are not the only means, though they are the chief, by which the black traders on the coast are supplied with negroes. Small parties of them, from five to ten, are frequently brought to the houses of the traders, by those who make a practice of kidnapping; and who are constantly employed in procuring a supply, while purchasers are to be found.

When the negroes, whom the black traders have to dispose of, are shewn to the European purchasers, they first examine them relative to their age. They then minutely inspect their persons, and inquire into the state of their health; if they are afflicted with any infirmity, or are deformed, or have bad eyes or teeth; if they are lame, or weak in the joints, or distorted in the back, or of a slender make, or are narrow in the chest; in short, if they have been, or are afflicted in any manner, so as to render them incapable of much labour; if any of the foregoing defects are discovered in them, they are rejected. But if approved of, they are generally taken on board the ship the same evening. The purchaser has liberty to return on the following morning, but not afterwards, such as upon re-examination are found exceptionable.

The traders frequently beat those negroes which are objected to by the captains, and use them with great severity. It matters not whether they are refused on account of age, illness, deformity, or for any other reason. At New Calabar, in particular, the traders have frequently been known to put them to death. Instances have happened at that place, that the traders, when any of their negroes have been objected to, have dropped their canoes under the stern of the vessel, and instantly beheaded them, in sight of the captain.

Upon the Windward Coast, another mode of procuring slaves is pursued; which is, by what they term *boating*; a mode that is very pernicious and destructive to the crews of the ships. The sailors, who are employed upon this trade, go in boats up the rivers, seeking for negroes, among the villages situated on the banks of them. But this method is very slow, and not always effectual. For, after being absent from the ship during a fortnight or three weeks, they sometimes return with only from eight to twelve negroes. Numbers of these are procured in consequence of alleged crimes, which, as before observed, whenever any ships are upon the coast, are more productive than at any other period. Kidnapping, however, prevails here.

I have good reason to believe, that of one hundred and twenty negroes, which were purchased for the ship to which I then belonged, then lying at the river Ambris, by far the greater part, if not the whole, were kidnapped. This, with various other instances, confirms me in the belief that kidnapping is the fund which supplies the thousands of negroes annually sold off these extensive Windward, and other Coasts, where boating prevails.

Treatment of the Slaves.

As soon as the wretched Africans, purchased at the fairs, fall into the hands of the black traders, they experience an earnest of those dreadful sufferings which they are doomed in future to undergo. And there is not the least room to doubt, but that even before they can reach the fairs, great numbers perish from cruel usage, want of food, travelling through inhospitable deserts, &c. They are brought from the places where they are purchased to Bonny, &c. in canoes; at the bottom of which they lie, having their hands tied with a kind of willow twigs, and a strict watch is kept over them. Their usage in other respects, during the time of the passage, which generally lasts several days, is equally cruel. Their allowance of food is so scanty, that it is barely sufficient to support nature. They are, besides, much exposed to the violent rains which frequently fall here, being covered only with mats that afford but a slight defence; and as there is usually water at the bottom of the canoes, from their leaking, they are scarcely ever dry.

Nor do these unhappy beings, after they become the property of the Europeans (from whom, as a more civilized people, more humanity might naturally be expected) find their situation in the least amended. Their treatment is no less rigorous. The men negroes, on being brought aboard the ship, are immediately fastened together, two and two, by hand-cuffs on their wrists, and by irons rivetted on their legs. They are then sent down between the decks, and placed in an apartment partitioned off for that purpose. The women likewise are placed in a separate apartment between decks, but without being ironed. And an adjoining room, on the same deck, is besides appointed for the boys. Thus are they all placed in different apartments.

But at the same time, they are frequently stowed so close, as to admit of no other posture than lying on their sides. Neither will the height between decks, unless directly under the grating, permit them the indulgence of an erect posture; especially where there are platforms, which is generally the case. These platforms are a kind of shelf, about eight or nine feet in breadth, extending from the side of the ship towards the centre. They are placed nearly midway between the decks, at the distance of two or three feet from each deck. Upon these the negroes are stowed in the same manner as they are on the deck underneath.

In each of the apartments are placed three or four large buckets, of a conical form, being near two feet in diameter at the bottom, and only one foot at the top, and in depth about twenty-eight inches; to which, when necessary, the negroes have recourse. It often happens, that those who are placed at a distance from the buckets, in endeavouring to get to them, tumble over their companions, in consequence of their being shackled. These accidents, although unavoidable, are productive of continual quarrels, in which some of them are always bruised. In this distressed situation, unable to proceed, and prevented from getting to the tubs, they desist from the attempt; and, as the necessities of nature are not to be repelled, ease themselves as they lie. This becomes a fresh source of broils and disturbances, and tends to render the condition of the poor captive wretches still more uncomfortable. The nuisance arising from these circumstances, is not unfrequently increased by the tubs being much too small for the purpose intended, and their being usually emptied but once every day. The rule for doing this, however, varies in different ships, according to the attention paid to the health and convenience of the slaves by the captain.

About eight o'clock in the morning the negroes are generally brought upon deck. Their irons being examined, a long chain, which is locked to a ring-bolt, fixed in the deck, is run through the rings of the shackles of the men, and then locked to another ring-bolt, fixed also in the deck. By this means fifty or sixty, and sometimes more, are fastened to one chain, in order to prevent them from rising, or endeavouring to escape. If the weather proves favourable, they are permitted to remain in that situation till four or five in the afternoon, when they are disengaged from the chain, and sent down.

The diet of the negroes, while on board, consists chiefly of horse-beans, boiled to the consistence of a pulp; of boiled yams and rice, and sometimes of a small quantity of beef or pork. The latter are frequently taken from the provisions laid in for the sailors. They sometimes make use of a sauce, composed of palm-oil, mixed with flour, water, and pepper, which the sailors call *slabber-sauce*. Yams are the favourite food of the Eboe, or Bight negroes, and rice or corn, of those from the Gold and Windward Coasts; each preferring the produce of their native soil.

In their own country, the negroes in general live on animal food and fish, with roots, yams, and Indian corn. The horse-beans and rice, with which they are fed aboard ship, are chiefly taken from Europe. The latter, indeed, is sometimes purchased on the coast, being far superior to any other.

The Gold Coast negroes scarcely ever refuse any food that is offered them, and they generally eat larger quantities of whatever is placed before them, than any other species of negroes, whom they likewise excel in strength of body and mind. Most of the slaves have such an aversion to the horse-beans, that unless they are narrowly watched, when fed upon deck, they will throw them overboard, or in each other's faces when they quarrel.

They are commonly fed twice a day, about eight o'clock in the morning and four in the afternoon. In most ships they are only fed with their *own food* once a day. Their food is served up to them in tubs, about the size of a small water bucket. They are placed round these tubs in companies of ten to each tub, out of which they feed themselves with wooden spoons. These they soon lose, and when they are not allowed others, they feed themselves with their hands. In favourable weather they are fed upon deck, but in bad weather their food is given them below. Numberless quarrels take place among them during their meals; more especially when they are put upon short allowance, which frequently happens, if the passage from the coast of Guinea to the West-India islands, proves of unusual length. In that case, the weak are obliged to be content with a very scanty portion. Their allowance of water is about half a pint each at every meal. It is handed round in a bucket, and given to each negroe in a pannekin; a small utensil with a strait handle, somewhat similar to a sauce-boat. However, when the ships approach the islands with a favourable breeze, they are no longer restricted.

Upon the negroes refusing to take sustenance, I have seen coals of fire, glowing hot, put on a shovel, and placed so near their lips, as to scorch and burn them. And this has been accompanied with threats, of forcing them to swallow the coals, if they any longer persisted in refusing to eat. These means have generally had the desired effect. I have also been credibly informed, that a certain captain in the slave trade, poured melted lead on such of the negroes as obstinately refused their food.

Exercise being deemed necessary for the preservation of their health, they are sometimes obliged to dance, when the weather will permit their coming on deck. If they go about it reluctantly, or do not move with agility, they are flogged; a person standing by them all the time with a cat-o'-nine-tails in his hand for that purpose. Their musick, upon these occasions, consists of a drum, sometimes with only one head; and when that is worn out, they do not scruple to make use of the bottom of one of the tubs before described. The poor wretches are frequently compelled to sing also; but when they do so, their songs are generally, as may naturally be expected, melancholy lamentations of their exile from their native country.

The women are furnished with beads for the purpose of affording them some diversion. But this end is generally defeated by the squabbles which are occasioned, in consequence of their stealing them from each other.

On board some ships, the common sailors are allowed to have intercourse with such of the black women whose consent they can procure. And some of them have been known to take the inconstancy of their paramours so much to heart, as to leap overboard and drown themselves. The officers are permitted to indulge their passions among them at pleasure, and sometimes are guilty of such brutal excesses, as disgrace human nature.

The hardships and inconveniencies suffered by the negroes during the passage, are scarcely to be enumerated or conceived. They are far more violently affected by the sea-sickness, than the Europeans. It frequently terminates in death, especially among the women. But the exclusion of the fresh air is among the most intolerable. For the purpose of admitting this needful refreshment, most of the ships in the slave-trade are provided, between the decks, with five or six air-ports on each side of the ship, of about six inches in length, and four in breadth; in addition to which, some few ships, but not one in twenty, have what they denominate *wind-sails*. But whenever the sea is rough, and the rain heavy, it becomes necessary to shut these, and every other conveyance by which the air is admitted. The fresh air being thus excluded, the negroes rooms very soon grow intolerably hot. The confined air, rendered noxious by the effluvia exhaled from their bodies, and by being repeatedly breathed, soon produces fevers and fluxes, which generally carries off great numbers of them.

During the voyages I made, I was frequently a witness to the fatal effects of this exclusion of the fresh air. I will give one instance, as it serves to convey some idea, though a very faint one, of the sufferings of those unhappy beings whom we wantonly drag from their native country, and doom to perpetual labour and captivity. Some wet and blowing weather having occasioned the port-holes to be shut, and the grating to be covered, fluxes and fevers among the negroes ensued. While they were in this situation, my profession requiring it, I frequently went down among them, till at length their apartments became so extremely hot, as to be only sufferable for a very short time. But the excessive heat was not the only thing that rendered their situation intolerable. The deck, that is, the floor of their rooms, was so covered with the blood and mucus which had proceeded from them in consequence of the flux, that it resembled a slaughter-house. It is not in the power of the human imagination, to picture to itself a situation more dreadful or disgusting. Numbers of the slaves having fainted, they were carried upon deck, where several of them died, and the rest were, with great difficulty, restored. It had nearly proved fatal to me also. The climate was too warm to admit the wearing of any clothing but a shirt, and that I had pulled off before I went down; notwithstanding which, by only continuing among them for about a quarter of an hour, I was so overcome with the heat, stench, and foul air, that I had nearly fainted; and it was not without assistance, that I could get upon deck. The consequence was, that I soon after fell sick of the same disorder, from which I did not recover for several months.

A circumstance of this kind, sometimes repeatedly happens in the course of a voyage; and often to a greater degree than what has just been described; particularly when the slaves are much crowded, which was not the case at that time, the ship having more than a hundred short of the number she was to have taken in.

This devastation, great as it was, some few years ago was greatly exceeded on board a Leverpool ship. I shall particularize the circumstances of it, as a more glaring instance of an insatiable thirst for gain, or of less attention to the lives and happiness even of that despised and oppressed race of mortals, the sable inhabitants of Africa, perhaps was never exceeded; though indeed several similar instances have been known.

This ship, though a much smaller ship than that in which the event I have just mentioned happened, took on board at Bonny, at least six hundred negroes; but according to the information of the black traders, from whom I received the intelligence immediately after the ship sailed, they amounted to near *seven hundred*. By purchasing so great a number, the slaves were so crowded, that they were even obliged to lie one upon another. This occasioned such a mortality among them, that, without meeting with unusual bad weather, or having a longer voyage than common, nearly one half of them died before the ship arrived in the West-Indies.

That the publick may be able to form some idea of the almost incredible small space into which so large a number of negroes were crammed, the following particulars of this ship are given. According to Leverpool custom she measured 235 tons. Her width across the beam, 25 feet. Length between the decks, 92 feet, which was divided into four rooms, thus:

Store room, in which there were not any negroes placed	15 feet
Negroes rooms—mens room—	about 45 feet
womens ditto	about 10 feet
boys ditto	about 22 feet
Total room for negroes	77 feet

Exclusive of the platform before described, from 8 to 9 feet in breadth, and equal in length to that of the rooms.

It may be worthy of remark, that the ships in this trade, are usually fitted out to receive only one third women negroes, or perhaps a smaller number, which the dimensions of the room allotted for them, above given, plainly shew, but in a greater disproportion.

One would naturally suppose, that an attention to their own interest, would prompt the owners of the Guinea ships not to suffer the captains to take on board a greater number of negroes than the ship would allow room sufficient for them to lie with ease to themselves, or, at least, without rubbing against each other. However that may be, a more striking instance than the above, of avarice, completely and deservedly disappointed, was surely never displayed; for there is little room to doubt, but that in consequence of the expected premium usually allowed to the captains, of 6*l.* per cent. sterling on the produce of the negroes, this vessel was so thronged as to occasion such a heavy loss.

The place allotted for the sick negroes is under the half deck, where they lie on the bare planks. By this means, those who are emaciated, frequently have their skin, and even their flesh, entirely rubbed off, by the motion of the ship, from the prominent parts of the shoulders, elbows, and hips, so as to render the bones in those parts quite bare. And some of them, by constantly lying in the blood and mucus, that had flowed from those afflicted with the flux, and which, as before observed, is generally so violent as to prevent their being kept clean, have their flesh much sooner rubbed off, than those who have only to contend with the mere friction of the ship. The excruciating pain which the poor sufferers feel from being obliged to continue in such a dreadful situation, frequently for several weeks, in case they happen to live so long, is not to be conceived or described. Few, indeed, are ever able to withstand the fatal effects of it. The utmost skill of the surgeon is here ineffectual. If plaisters be applied, they are very soon displaced by the friction of the ship; and when bandages are used, the negroes very soon take them off, and appropriate them to other purposes.

The surgeon, upon going between decks, in the morning, to examine the situation of the slaves, frequently finds several dead; and among the men, sometimes a dead and living negroe fastened by their irons together. When this is the case, they are brought upon the deck, and being laid on the grating, the living negroe is disengaged, and the dead one thrown overboard.

It may not be improper here to remark, that the surgeons employed in the Guinea trade, are generally driven to engage in so disagreeable an employ by the confined state of their finances. An exertion of the greatest skill and attention could afford the diseased negroes little relief, so long as the causes of their diseases, namely, the breathing of a putrid atmosphere, and wallowing in their own excrements, remain. When once the fever and dysentery get to any height at sea, a cure is scarcely ever effected.

Almost the only means by which the surgeon can render himself useful to the slaves, is, by seeing that their food is properly cooked, and distributed among them. It is true, when they arrive near the markets for which they are destined, care is taken to polish them for sale, by an application of the lunar caustic to such as are afflicted with the yaws. This, however, affords but a temporary relief, as the disease most assuredly breaks out, whenever the patient is put upon a vegetable diet.

It has been asserted, in favour of the captains in this trade, that the sick slaves are usually fed from their tables. The great number generally ill at a time, proves the falsity of such an assertion. Were even a captain *disposed* to do this, how could he feed half the slaves in the ship from his own table? for it is well known, that *more than half* are often sick at a time. Two or three perhaps may be fed.

The loss of slaves, through mortality, arising from the causes just mentioned, are frequently very considerable. In the voyage lately referred to (not the Leverpool ship before-mentioned) one hundred and five, out of three hundred and eighty, died in the passage. A proportion seemingly very great, but by no means uncommon. One half, sometimes two thirds, and even beyond that, have been known to perish. Before we left Bonny River, no less than fifteen died of fevers and dysenteries, occasioned by their confinement. On the Windward Coast, where slaves are procured more slowly, very few die, in proportion to the numbers which die at Bonny, and at Old and New Calabar, where they are obtained much faster; the latter being of a more delicate make and habit.

The havock made among the seamen engaged in this destructive commerce, will be noticed in another part; and will be found to make no inconsiderable addition to the unnecessary waste of life just represented.

As very few of the negroes can so far brook the loss of their liberty, and the hardships they endure, as to bear them with any degree of patience, they are ever upon the watch to take advantage of the least negligence in their oppressors. Insurrections are frequently the consequence; which are seldom suppressed without much bloodshed. Sometimes these are successful, and the whole ship's company is cut off. They are likewise always ready to seize every opportunity for committing some act of desperation to free themselves from their miserable state; and notwithstanding the restraints under which they are laid, they often succeed.

While a ship, to which I belonged, lay in Bonny River, one evening, a short time before our departure, a lot of negroes, consisting of about ten, was brought on board; when one of them, in a favourable moment, forced his way through the net-work on the larboard side of the vessel, jumped overboard, and was supposed to have been devoured by the sharks.

During the time we were there, fifteen negroes belonging to a vessel from Leverpool, found means to throw themselves into the river; very few were saved; and the residue fell a sacrifice to the sharks. A similar instance took place in a French ship while we lay there.

Circumstances of this kind are very frequent. On the coast of Angola, at the River Ambris, the following incident happened:——During the time of our residing on shore, we erected a tent to shelter ourselves from the weather. After having been there several weeks, and being unable to purchase the number of slaves we wanted, through the opposition of another English slave vessel, we determined to leave the place. The night before our departure, the tent was struck; which was no sooner perceived by some of the negroe women on board, than it was considered as a prelude to our sailing; and about eighteen of them, when they were sent between decks, threw themselves into the sea through one of the gun ports; the ship carrying guns between decks. They were all of them, however, excepting one, soon picked up; and that which was missing, was, not long after, taken about a mile from the shore.

I once knew a negroe woman, too sensible of her woes, who pined for a considerable time, and was taken ill of a fever and dysentery; when declaring it to be her determination to die, she refused all food and medical aid, and, in about a fortnight after, expired. On being thrown overboard, her body was instantly torn to pieces by the sharks.

The following circumstance also came within my knowledge. A young female negroe, falling into a desponding way, it was judged necessary, in order to attempt her recovery, to send her on shore, to the hut of one of the black traders. Elevated with the prospect of regaining her liberty by this unexpected step, she soon recovered her usual chearfulness; but hearing, by accident, that it was intended to take her on board the ship again, the poor young creature hung herself.

It frequently happens that the negroes, on being purchased by the Europeans, become raving mad; and many of them die in that state; particularly the women. While I was one day ashore at Bonny, I saw a middle aged stout woman, who had been brought down from a fair the preceding day, chained to the post of a black trader's door, in a state of furious insanity. On board a ship in Bonny River, I saw a young negroe woman chained to the deck, who had lost her senses, soon after she was purchased and taken on board. In a former voyage, on board a ship to which I belonged, we were obliged to confine a female negroe, of about twenty-three years of age, on her becoming a lunatic. She was afterwards sold during one of her lucid intervals.

One morning, upon examining the place allotted for the sick negroes, I perceived that one of them, who was so emaciated as scarcely to be able to walk, was missing, and was convinced that he must have gone overboard in the night, probably to put a more expeditious period to his sufferings. And, to conclude on this subject, I could not help being sensibly affected, on a former voyage, at observing with what apparent eagerness a black woman seized some dirt from off an African yam, and put it into her mouth; seeming to rejoice at the opportunity of possessing some of her native earth.

From these instances I think it may be clearly deduced, that the unhappy Africans are not bereft of the finer feelings, but have a strong attachment to their native country, together with a just sense of the value of liberty. And the situation of the miserable beings above described, more forcibly urge the necessity of abolishing a trade which is the source of such evils, than the most eloquent harangue, or persuasive arguments could do.

Sale of the Slaves.

When the ships arrive in the West-Indies, (the chief mart for this inhuman merchandize), the slaves are disposed of, as I have before observed, by different methods. Sometimes the mode of disposal, is that of selling them by what is termed a *scramble*; and a day is soon fixed for that purpose. But previous thereto, the sick, or refuse slaves, of which there are frequently many, are usually conveyed on shore, and sold at a tavern by vendue, or public auction. These, in general, are purchased by the Jews and surgeons, but chiefly the former, upon speculation, at so low a price as five or six dollars a head. I was informed by a mulatto woman, that she purchased a sick slave at Grenada, upon speculation, for the small sum of one dollar, as the poor wretch was apparently dying of the flux. It seldom happens that any, who are carried ashore in the emaciated state to which they are generally reduced by that disorder, long survive their landing. I once saw sixteen conveyed on shore, and sold in the foregoing manner, the whole of whom died before I left the island, which was within a short time after. Sometimes the captains march their slaves through the town at which they intend to dispose of them; and then place them in rows where they are examined and purchased.

The mode of selling them by scramble having fallen under my observation the oftenest, I shall be more particular in describing it. Being some years ago, at one of the islands in the West-Indies, I was witness to a sale by scramble, where about 250 negroes were sold. Upon this occasion all the negroes scrambled for bear an equal price; which is agreed upon between the captains and the purchasers before the sale begins.

On a day appointed, the negroes were landed, and placed altogether in a large yard, belonging to the merchants to whom the ship was consigned. As soon as the hour agreed on arrived, the doors of the yard were suddenly thrown open, and in rushed a considerable number of purchasers, with all the ferocity of brutes. Some instantly seized such of the negroes as they could conveniently lay hold of with their hands. Others, being prepared with several handkerchiefs tied together, encircled with these as many as they were able. While others, by means of a rope, effected the same purpose. It is scarcely possible to describe the confusion of which this mode of selling is productive. It likewise causes much animosity among the purchasers, who, not unfrequently upon these occasions, fall out and quarrel with each other. The poor astonished negroes were so much terrified by these proceedings, that several of them, through fear, climbed over the walls of the court yard, and ran wild about the town; but were soon hunted down and retaken.

While on a former voyage from Africa to Kingston in Jamaica, I saw a sale there by scramble, on board a snow. The negroes were collected together upon the main and quarter decks, and the ship was darkened by sails suspended over them, in order to prevent the purchasers from being able to see, so as to pick or chuse. The signal being given, the buyers rushed in, as usual, to seize their prey; when the negroes appeared to be extremely terrified, and near thirty of them jumped into the sea. But they were all soon retaken, chiefly by boats from other ships.

On board a ship, lying at Port Maria, in Jamaica, I saw another scramble; in which, as usual, the poor negroes were greatly terrified. The women, in particular, clang to each other in agonies scarcely to be conceived, shrieking through excess of terror, at the savage manner in which their brutal purchasers rushed upon, and seized them. Though humanity, one should imagine, would dictate the captains to apprize the poor negroes of the mode by which they were to be sold, and by that means to guard them, in some degree, against the surprize and terror which must attend it, I never knew that any notice of the scramble was given to them. Nor have I any reason to think that it is done; or that this mode of sale is less frequent at this time, than formerly.

Various are the deceptions made use of in the disposal of the sick slaves; and many of these, such as must excite in every humane mind, the liveliest sensations of horror. I have been well informed, that a Liverpool captain boasted of his having cheated some Jews by the following stratagem: A lot of slaves, afflicted with the flux, being about to be landed for sale, he directed the surgeon to stop the anus of each of them with oakum. Thus prepared, they were landed, and taken to the accustomed place of sale; where, being unable to stand but for a very short time, they are usually permitted to sit. The Jews, when they examine them, oblige them to stand up, in order to see if there be any discharge; and when they do not perceive this appearance, they consider it as a symptom of recovery. In the present instance, such an appearance being prevented, the bargain was struck, and they were accordingly sold. But it was not long before a discovery ensued. The excruciating pain which the prevention of a discharge of such an acrimonious nature occasioned, not being to be borne by the poor wretches, the temporary obstruction was removed, and the deluded purchasers were speedily convinced of the imposition.

So grievously are the negroes sometimes afflicted with this troublesome and painful disorder, that I have seen large numbers of them, after being landed, obliged by the virulence of the complaint, to stop almost every minute, as they passed on.

Treatment of the Sailors.

The evils attendant on this inhuman traffick, are not confined to the purchased negroes. The sufferings of the seamen employed in the slave-trade, from the unwholesomeness of the climate, the inconveniences of the voyage, the brutal severity of the commanders, and other causes, fall very little short, nor prove in proportion to the numbers, less destructive to the sailors than negroes.

The sailors on board the Guinea ships, are not allowed always an equal quantity of beef and pork with those belonging to other merchant ships. In these articles they are frequently much stinted, particularly when the negroes are on board; part of the stock laid in for the sailors, being, as before observed, appropriated to their use.

With regard to their drink, they are generally denied grog, and are seldom allowed any thing but water to quench their thirst. This urges them, when opportunity offers, at Bonny and other places on the coast, to barter their clothes with the natives, for English brandy, which the Africans obtain, among other articles, in exchange for slaves; and they frequently leave themselves nearly naked, in order to indulge an excess in spiritous liquors. In this state, they are often found lying on the deck, and in different parts of the ship, exposed to the heavy dews which in those climates fall during the night; notwithstanding the deck is usually washed every evening. This frequently causes pains in the head and limbs, accompanied with a fever, which generally, in the course of a few days, occasions their death.

The temporary house constructed on the deck, affords but an indifferent shelter from the weather; yet the sailors are obliged to lodge under it, as all the parts between decks are occupied by, or kept for, the negroes. The cabin is frequently full, and when this is the case, or the captain finds the heat and the stench intolerable, he quits his cot, which is usually hung over the slaves, and sleeps in the round-house, if there be one, as there is in many ships.

The foul air that arises from the negroes when they are much crowded, is very noxious to the crew; and this is not a little increased by the additional heat which the covering over the ship occasions. The mangrove smoke is likewise, as before observed, productive of disorders among them.

Nor are they better accommodated after they leave the Coast of Africa. During the whole of the passage to the West-Indies, which in general lasts seven weeks, or two months, they are obliged, for want of room between decks, to keep upon deck. This exposure to the weather, is also found very prejudicial to the health of the sailors, and frequently occasions fevers, which generally prove fatal. The only resemblance of a shelter, is a tarpawling thrown over the booms, which even before they leave the coast, is generally so full of holes, as to afford scarce any defence against the wind or the rain, of which a considerable quantity usually falls during this passage.

Many other causes contribute to affect the health of the sailors. The water at Bonny, which they are obliged to drink, is very unwholesome; and, together with their scanty and bad diet, and the cruel usage they receive from the officers, tends to impoverish the blood, and render them extremely susceptible of putrid fevers and dysenteries.

The seamen, whose health happen to be impaired, are discharged, on the arrival of the ships in the West-Indies, and as soon as they get ashore, they have recourse to spiritous liquors, to which they are the more prone, on account of having been denied grog, or even any liquor but water, during their being aboard; the consequence of which is, a certain and speedy destruction. Numbers likewise die in the West-India islands, of the scurvy, brought on in consequence of poverty of diet, and exposure to all weathers.

I am now come to a part of the sufferings of the sailors who are employed in the slave-trade, of which, for the honour of human nature, I would willingly decline giving an account; that is, the treatment they receive from their officers, which makes no inconsiderable addition to the hardships and ailments just mentioned, and contributes not a little to rob the nation annually, of a considerable number of this valuable body of men. However, as truth demands, and the occasion requires it, I will relate some of the circumstances of this kind, which fell under my own immediate observation, during the several voyages I made in that line.

In one of these, I was witness to the following instance of cruel usage. Most of the sailors were treated with brutal severity; but one in particular, a man advanced in years, experienced it in an uncommon degree. Having made some complaint relative to his allowance of water, and this being construed into an insult, one of the officers seized him, and with the blows he bestowed upon him, beat out several of his teeth. Not content with this, while the poor old man was yet bleeding, one of the iron pump-bolts was fixed in his mouth, and kept there by a piece of rope-yarn tied round his head. Being unable to spit out the blood which flowed from the wound, the man was almost choaked, and obliged to swallow it. He was then tied to the rail of the quarter-deck, having declared, upon being gagged, that he would jump overboard and drown himself. About two hours after he was taken from the quarter-deck rail, and fastened to the grating companion of the steerage, under the half deck, where he remained all night with a centinel placed over him.

A young man on board one of the ships, was frequently beaten in a very severe manner, for very trifling faults. This was done sometimes with what is termed *a cat*, (an instrument of correction, which consists of a handle or stem, made of a rope three inches and a half in circumference, and about eighteen inches in length, at one of which are fastened nine branches, or tails, composed of log line, with three or more knots upon each branch), and sometimes he was beat with a bamboo. Being one day cruelly beaten with the latter, the poor lad, unable to endure the severe usage, leaped out of one of the gun ports on the larboard side of the cabin, into the river. He, however, providentially escaped being devoured by the sharks, and was taken up by a canoe belonging to one of the black traders then lying along-side the vessel. As soon as he was brought on board, he was dragged to the quarter-deck, and his head forced into a tub of water, which had been left there for the negroe women to wash their hands in. In this situation he was kept till he was nearly suffocated; the person who held him, exclaiming, with the malignity of a demon, "If you want drowning, I will drown you myself." Upon my inquiring of the young man, if he knew the danger to which he exposed himself by jumping overboard, he replied, "that he expected to be devoured by the sharks, but he preferred even that, to being treated daily with so much cruelty."

Another seaman having been in some degree negligent, had a long chain fixed round his neck, at the end of which was fastened a log of wood. In this situation he performed his duty, (from which he was not in the least spared) for several weeks, till at length he was nearly exhausted by fatigue; and after his release from the log, he was frequently beaten for trivial faults. Once, in particular, when an accident happened, through the carelessness of another seaman, he was tied up, although the fault was not in the least imputable to him, along with the other person, and they were both flogged till their backs were raw. Chian pepper was then mixed in a bucket, with salt water, and with this the harrowed parts of the back of the unoffending seaman were washed, as an addition to his torture.

The same seaman having at another time accidentally broken a plate, a fish-gig was thrown at him with great violence. The fish-gig is an instrument used for striking fish, and consists of several strong barbed points fixed on a pole, about six feet long, loaded at the end with lead. The man escaped the threatening danger, by stooping his head, and the missile weapon struck in the barricado. Knives and forks were at other times thrown at him; and a large Newfoundland dog was frequently set at him, which, thus encouraged, would not only tear his cloths, but wound him. At length, after several severe floggings, and other ill treatment, the poor fellow appeared to be totally insensible to beating, and careless of the event.

I must here add, that whenever any of the crew were beaten, the Newfoundland dog, just mentioned, from the encouragement he met with, would generally leap upon them, tear their cloths, and bite them. He was particularly inveterate against one of the seamen, who, from being often knocked down, and severely beaten, appeared quite stupid, and incapable of doing his duty. In this state, he was taken on board another ship, and returned to England.

In one of my voyages, a seaman came on board the ship I belonged to, while on the coast, as a passenger to the West-Indies. He was just recovered from a fever, and notwithstanding this, he was very unmercifully beaten during the passage, which, together with the feeble state he was in at the time, rendered him nearly incapable of walking, and it was but by stealth, that any medical assistance could be given to him.

A young man was likewise beaten and kicked almost daily, for trifling, and even imaginary faults. The poor youth happening to have a very bad toe, through a hurt, he was placed as a centry over the sick slaves, a station which required much walking. This, in addition to the pain it occasioned, increased a fever he already had. Soon after he was compelled, although so ill, to sit on the gratings, and being there overcome with illness and fatigue, he chanced to fall asleep; which being observed from the quarter-deck, he was soon awakened, and with many oaths, upbraided for neglect of duty. He was then kicked from the gratings, and so cruelly beaten, that it was with great difficulty he crawled to one of the officers who was more humane, and complaining of the cruel treatment he had just received, petitioned for a little barley-water (which was kept for the sick slaves) to quench the intolerable thirst he experienced.

Another seaman was knocked down several times a day, for faults of no deep dye. It being observed at one time, that the hen coops had not been removed by the sailors who were then washing the deck, nor washed under, which it was his duty to see done, one of the officers immediately knocked him down, then seized and dragged him to the stern of the vessel, where he threw him violently against the deck. By this treatment, various parts of his body was much bruised, his face swelled, and he had a bad eye for a fortnight. He was afterwards severely beaten for a very trifling fault, and kicked till he fell down. When he got on shore in the West-Indies, he carried his shirt, stained with the blood which had flowed from his wounds, to one of the magistrates of the island, and applied to him for redress; but the ship being consigned to one of them, all the redress he could procure, was his discharge.

Many other instances of similar severity might be produced; but the foregoing will suffice, to give some idea of the treatment seamen are liable to, and generally experience, in this employ; the consequence of which usually is desertion or death.

Of the former I will give one instance. While a ship I belonged to lay at Bonny, early one morning near a dozen of the crew deserted in one of the long boats. They were driven to this desperate measure, as one of them afterwards informed me, by the cruel treatment they had experienced on board. Two of them, in particular, had been severely beaten and flogged the preceding day. One of these having neglected to see that the arms of the ship were kept fit for use, was tied up to the mizen shrouds, and after being stripped, very severely flogged on the back; his trowsers were then pulled down, and the floging was repeated. The other seaman, who was esteemed a careful, cleanly, sober fellow, had been punished little less severely, though it did not appear that he had been guilty at that time of any fault.

It is customary for most of the captains of the slave ships to go on shore every evening to do business with the black traders. Upon these occasions many of them get intoxicated, and when they return on board, give proofs of their inebriation, by beating and ill using some or other of the crew. This was the present case; the seaman here spoken of, was beaten, without any reason being assigned, with a knotted bamboo, for a considerable time; by which he was very much bruised, and being before in an ill state of health, suffered considerably.

Irritated by the ill usage which all of them, in their turn, had experienced, they resolved to attempt an escape, and effected it early in the morning. The person on the watch discovered, that the net-work on the main deck had been cut, and that one of the long-boats was gone; and, upon farther examination it was found, that near a dozen of the seamen were missing. A few hours after, the captain went in the cutter in pursuit of the deserters, but without success.

On my return to England, I received from one of them, the following account of their adventures during this undertaking.

When they left the vessel, they proposed going to Old Calabar, being determined to perish, rather than return to the ship. All the provisions they took with them was, a bag containing about half a hundred weight of bread, half a small cheese, and a cask of water of about 38 gallons. They made a sail of a hammock, and erected one of the boat's oars for a mast. Thus slenderly provided, they dropped down the river of Bonny, and kept along the coast; but mistaking one river for another, they were seized by the natives, who stripped them, and marched them across the country, for a considerable distance, to the place to which they themselves intended going. During the march, several were taken ill, and some of them died. Those who survived, were sold to an English ship which lay there. Every one of these deserters, except three, died on the coast, or during their passage to the West-Indies; and one of the remaining three died soon after his arrival there. So that only two out of the whole number, lived to arrive in England, and those in a very infirm state of health.

While I am upon the subject of the desertions among the sailors, I must add, that the captains in this trade generally take out with them tobacco and slops, which they sell at an exorbitant price to the sailors. And in case of their desertion or decease, they have it in their power to charge to the seamens accounts, whatever quantity they please, without contradiction. This proves an additional reason for cruel usage. In case of desertion, the sailors forfeit their wages, by which the expences of the voyage are lessened, and consequently the merchants reap benefit from it.

The relation just given of the barbarities exercised by the officers in the slave trade, upon the seamen under their command, may appear to those who are unacquainted with the method in which this iniquitous branch of commerce is conducted, to be exaggerated. But I can assure them, that every instance is confined within the strictest bounds of truth. Many others may likewise be brought to prove, that those I have recited are by no means singular. Indeed, the reverse of this conduct would be esteemed a singularity. For the common practice of the officers in the Guinea trade, I am sorry to say it, will, with a very few exceptions, justify the assertion, that to harden the feelings, and to inspire a *delight in giving torture* to a fellow creature, is the natural tendency of this unwarrantable traffick. It is but justice however, that I except from this general censure, one captain with whom I sailed. Upon all occasions I found him to be a humane and considerate man, and ever ready to alleviate the evils attendant on the trade, as far as they were to be lessened.

The annual diminution of British seamen by all the foregoing causes, is what next claims attention, and upon due investigation will be found, I fear, to be much more considerable than it is generally supposed to be. As this is a question of great national importance, and cannot fail to evince the necessity of an abolition of the slave trade; in order to convey to the public some idea of the destructive tendency of it, I will give an account of the statement of the loss of a ship, to which I belonged, during one of her voyages. And though this statement may not be considered as an average of the loss upon each voyage, which I have before estimated, as I would not wish to exceed the mark, at one fourth, and oftentimes one third. I have known instances where it has been greatly exceeded, as I shall presently shew.

The crew of the ship I speak of, upon its departure from England, consisted of forty-six persons, exclusive of the captain, chief mate, and myself. Out of this number, we lost on the coast eleven by desertion (of whom only two, and those in a very infirm state, ever arrived in England) and five by death. Three perished in the middle passage, of whom one was a passenger. In the West-Indies, two died, one of which was a passenger from Bonny. Five were discharged at their own request, having been cruelly treated, and five deserted, exclusive of two who shipped themselves at Bonny; of these ten, several were in a diseased state; and probably, like most of the seamen who are discharged or desert from the Guinea ships in the islands, never returned to their native country. One died in our passage from the West-Indies to England; and one, having been rendered incapable of duty, was sent on board another ship while we lay at Bonny.

Thus, out of the forty-six persons before-mentioned, only fifteen returned home in the ship. And several, out of this small number, so enervated in their constitution, as to be of little service in future; they were, on the contrary, reduced to the mournful necessity of becoming burthensome to themselves and to others. Of the ten that deserted, or were discharged in the West-Indies, little account can be taken; it being extremely improbable that one half, perhaps not a third, ever returned to this country.

From hence it appears, that there was a loss in this voyage of thirty-one sailors and upwards, exclusive of the two sailors who were passengers, and not included in the ship's crew. I say *a loss of thirty-one*, for though the whole of this number did not die, yet if it be considered, that several of those who returned to England in the ship, or who might have returned by other ships, are likely to become a burthen, instead of being useful to the community, it will be readily acknowledged, I doubt not, that the foregoing statement does not exceed reality.

How worthy of serious consideration is the diminution here represented, of a body of people so valuable in a commercial state! But how much more alarming will this be, when it appears, as is really the case, that the loss of seamen in the voyage I am speaking of, is not equal to what is experienced even by some other ships trading to Bonny and Calabar; and much less than by those employed in boating on the Windward Coast; where frequently there happens such a mortality among the crew, as not to leave a sufficient number of hands to navigate the ships to the West-Indies. In the year 1786, I saw a ship, belonging to Miles Barber, and Co. at Cape Monserado, on the Windward Coast, which had lost all the crew except three, from *boating*; a practice that proves extremely destructive to sailors, by exposing them to the parching sun and heavy dews of Africa, for weeks together, while they are seeking for negroes up the rivers, as before described.

It might naturally be asked, as such are the dangers to which the sailors employed in the slave trade are exposed from the intemperature of the climate, the inconveniencies of the voyage, and the treatment of the officers, how the captains are able to procure a sufficient number to man their ships. I answer, that it is done by a series of finesse and imposition, aided not only by allurements, but by threats.

There are certain public-houses, in which, for interested purposes, the sailors are trusted, and encouraged to run in debt. To the landlords of these houses the captains apply. And a certain number being fixed on, the landlord immediately insists upon their entering on board such a ship, threatening, in case of refusal, to arrest and throw them into prison. At the same time the captain holds out the allurements of a month's pay in advance above the ships in any other trade, and the promise of satisfying their inexorable landlords. Thus terrified on the one hand by the apprehensions of a prison, and allured on the other by the promised advance, they enter. And by this means a very great proportion of the sailors in the slave trade are procured; only a very small number of landmen are employed. During the several voyages I have been in the trade, I have not known the number to exceed one for each voyage. The few ships that go out in time of war, generally take with them, as other merchant ships do, a greater proportion of landmen. And with regard to apprentices, we had not any on board the ships I sailed in, neither to my knowledge have I ever seen any. So far is this trade from proving a nursery for seamen.

By their articles, on entering on board some Guinea ships, the sailors are restrained, under forfeiture of their wages, from applying, in case of ill usage, to any one for redress, except to such persons as shall be nominated by the owners or the captain; and by others, to commence an action against the captain for bad treatment, incurs a penalty of fifty pounds. These restrictions seem to be a tacit acknowledgment on the part of the owners and captains, that ill treatment is to be expected.

Having stated the foregoing facts relative to the nature of this destructive and inhuman traffick, I shall leave those, whose more immediate business it is, to deduce the necessary conclusions; and shall proceed to give a few cursory observations on those parts of the coast of Africa already referred to; confining myself to such as tend to an elucidation of the slave trade, without entering minutely into the state of the country.

A short Description of such Parts of the Coast of Guinea, as are before referred to.

BONNY, or BANNY, is a large town situate in the Bight of Benin, on the coast of Guinea, lying about twelve miles from the sea, on the east side of a river of the same name, opposite to a town called Peter-forte-side. It consists of a considerable number of very poor huts, built of upright poles, plaistered with a kind of red earth, and covered with mats. They are very low, being only one story. The floor is made of sand, which being constructed on swampy ground, does not long retain its firmness, but requires frequent repair.

The inhabitants secure themselves, in some degree, against the noxious vapours, which arise from the swamps and woods that surround the town, by constantly keeping large wood fires in their huts. They are extremely dirty and indolent; which, together with what they call the *smokes*, (a noxious vapour, arising from the swamps about the latter end of autumn) produces an epidemical fever, that carries off great numbers.

The natives of Bonny believe in one Supreme Being; but they reverence greatly a harmless animal of the lizard kind, called a Guana, the body of which is about the size of a man's leg, and tapering towards its tail, nearly to a point. Great numbers of them run about the town, being encouraged and cherished by the inhabitants.

The river of Bonny abounds with sharks of a very large size, which are often seen in almost incredible numbers about the slave ships, devouring with great dispatch the dead bodies of the negroes as they are thrown overboard. The bodies of the sailors who die there, are buried on a sandy point, called Bonny Point, which lies about a quarter of a mile from the town. It is covered at high water; and, as the bodies are buried but a small depth below the surface of the sand, the stench arising from them is sometimes very noxious.

The trade of this town consists of slaves, and a small quantity of ivory and palm-oil, the latter of which the inhabitants use as we do butter; but its chief dependence is on the slave trade, in which it exceeds any other place on the coast of Africa. The only water here is rain-water, which stagnating in a dirty pool, is very unwholesome. With this, as there is no better to be procured, the ships are obliged to supply themselves, though, when drank by the sailors, it frequently occasions violent pains in the bowels, accompanied with a diarrhæa.

THE WINDWARD COAST of Africa has a very beautiful appearance from the sea, being covered with trees, which are green all the year. It produces rice, cotton, and indigo of the first quality, and likewise a variety of roots, such as yams, casava, sweet potatoes, &c. &c. The soil is very rich, and the rice which it produces, is superior to that of Carolina; the cotton also is very fine. It has a number of fine rivers, that are navigable for small sloops, a considerable way up the country.

The natives are a strong hardy race, especially about Setrecrou, where they are always employed in hunting and fishing. They are extremely athletic and muscular, and are very expert in the water, and can swim for many miles. They can likewise dive to almost any depth. I have often thrown pieces of iron and tobacco pipes overboard, which they have never failed bringing up in their hand.

Their canoes are very small, not weighing above twenty-eight pounds each, and seldom carrying above two or three people. It is surprizing to see with what rapidity they paddle themselves through the water, and to what a distance they venture in them from the shore. I have seen them eight or nine miles distant from it. In stormy weather the sea frequently fills them, which the persons in them seem to disregard. When this happens, they leap into the sea, and taking hold of the ends of the canoe, turn her over several times, till they have emptied her of the chief part of the water; they then get in again, with great agility, and throw out the remainder with a small scoop, made for that purpose.

They sell some ivory and Malegetta pepper.

They are very cleanly in their houses, as likewise in cooking their victuals. The ivory on this coast is very fine, especially at Cape Lahoe. There are on this coast small cattle.

THE GOLD COAST has not so pleasing an appearance from the sea, as the Windward coast; but the natives are full as hardy, if not more so. The reason given for this is, that as their country is not so fertile as the Windward Coast, they are obliged to labour more in the cultivation of rice and corn, which is their chief food. They have here, as on the Windward Coast, hogs, goats, fowls, and abundance of fine fish, &c. They are very fond of brandy, and always get intoxicated when it is in their power to do so. They are likewise very bold and resolute, and insurrections happen more frequently among them, when on ship-board, than amongst the negroes of any other part of the coast.

The trade here is carried on by means of gold-dust, for which the Europeans give them goods, such as pieces of India chintz, bafts, romals, guns, powder, tobacco, brandy, pewter, iron, lead, copper, knives, &c. &c. After the gold dust is purchased, it is again disposed of to the natives for negroes. Their mode of reckoning in this traffick, is by ounces; thus they say they will have so many ounces for a slave; and according to the number of ships on the coast, the price of these differs.

The English have several forts on the Gold Coast, the principle of which are, Cape Corse, and Anamaboe. The trade carried on at these forts, is bartering for negroes, which the governors sell again to the European ships, for the articles before-mentioned.

The natives, as just observed, are a bold, resolute people. During the last voyage I was upon the coast, I saw a number of negroes in Cape Corse Castle, some of whom were part of the cargo of a ship from London, on whose crew they had risen, and, after killing the captain and most of the sailors, ran the ship on shore; but in endeavouring to make their escape, most of them were seized by the natives, and resold. Eighteen of these we purchased from Governor Morgue. The Dutch have likewise a strong fort on this coast, called Elmina, where they carry on a considerable trade for slaves.

The principal places of trade for negroes, are Bonny and Calabar. The town and trade of Bonny, I have already described. That of Calabar is nearly similar. The natives of the latter are of a much more delicate frame than those of the Windward and Gold Coasts.

The natives of Angola are the mildest, and most expert in mechanicks, of any of the Africans. Their country is the most plentiful of any in those parts, and produces different sorts of grain, particularly calavances, of which they seem, when on ship-board, to be extremely fond. Here are likewise hogs, sheep, goats, fowls, &c. in great abundance, insomuch, that when I was at the River Ambris, we could buy a fine fat sheep for a small keg of gunpowder, the value of which was about one shilling and sixpence sterling. They have also great plenty of fine fish. I have often seen turtle caught, while fishing with a net for other fish. They have a species of wild cinnamon, which has a very pungent taste in the mouth. The soil seems extremely rich, and the vegetation luxuriant and quick. A person might walk for miles in the country amidst wild jessamin trees.

The Portuguese have a large town on this coast, named St. Paul's, the inhabitants of which, and of the country for many miles round, profess the

Roman Catholick religion. They are in general strictly honest. The town of St. Paul's is strongly fortified, and the Portuguese do not suffer any other nation to trade there.

THE END.